Diplodocus

Daniel Nunn

raintree

a Capstone company — publishers for children

Raintree is an imprint of Capstone Global Library Limited, a company incorporated in England and Wales having its registered office at 7 Pilgrim Street, London, EC4V 6LB – Registered company number: 6695582

www.raintreepublishers.co.uk
myorders@raintreepublishers.co.uk

Text © Capstone Global Library Limited 2015
First published in paperback in 2016
The moral rights of the proprietor have been asserted.

Edited by Daniel Nunn and James Benefield
Designed by Tim Bond
Picture research by Tracy Cummins
Production by Helen McCreath
Originated by Capstone Global Library Ltd
Printed and bound in China

ISBN 978 1 4062 8085 2
18 17 16 15 14
10 9 8 7 6 5 4 3 2 1

ISBN 978 1 4062 8092 0 (paperback)
19 18 17 16 15
10 9 8 7 6 5 4 3 2 1

British Library Cataloguing in Publication Data
A full catalogue record for this book is available from the British Library.

Acknowledgements
We would like to thank the following for permission to reproduce photographs: Alamy pp. 5a (© blickwinkel), 10, 11 (© vario images GmbH & Co.KG), 21 (© andy lane); istockphoto pp. 5c (© PaulTessier), 7 bottom (© JeffBanke); Science Source p. 20 (Francois Gohier); Shutterstock pp. 4, 8 left, 12, 13 (Catmando), 5b, 23 (JASON STEEL), 5d (ProteinRobot), 6 (Michael Rosskothen), 7 top (Linda Bucklin), 8 right (Mikhail Tchkheidze), 8 scale (Pixel-3D), 9 (Christian Darkin), 16 (Matteo Volpone); Superstock pp. 14, 17 (Stocktrek Images), 15, 19 (NHPA), 18, 23 (Album / Prisma / Album).

Cover photograph of Diplodocus (Computer generated 3D illustration) reproduced with permission of Shutterstock (Michael Rosskothen).

Back cover photograph of Diplodocus reproduced with permission of Shutterstock(Michael Rosskothen).

We would like to thank Dee Reid and Nancy Harris for their invaluable help in the preparation of this book.

Every effort has been made to contact copyright holders of material reproduced in this book. Any omissions will be rectified in subsequent printings if notice is given to the publisher.

Contents

Meet Diplodocus

Diplodocus was a dinosaur.

Dinosaurs lived long ago.

dinosaur

snake

crocodile

lizard

Dinosaurs were reptiles.
Snakes, crocodiles and lizards
are reptiles that live today.

5

What was Diplodocus like?

Diplodocus was a very big dinosaur.

Diplodocus was as long as five elephants standing in a line!

Diplodocus was as heavy
as a lorry!

Diplodocus had strong legs.

Diplodocus had
a very long neck.

Diplodocus ate plants.

Diplodocus had to eat all day to get enough food!

tail

Diplodocus had a very long tail.

Other dinosaurs tried to eat
Diplodocus.

Diplodocus used its tail
to fight back.

Where is Diplodocus now?

Diplodocus is extinct. There are no Diplodocus alive now.

All the dinosaurs died long ago.

We learn about Diplodocus
from fossils.

fossil

Fossils are animal bones that have turned to rock.

People find fossils in the ground.

Fossils show us what Diplodocus looked like.

Where in the world?

Diplodocus fossils have
been found in North America.

Picture glossary

 **fossil** animal bones or parts of a plant that have turned into rock

 **reptile** cold-blooded animal. A snake is a reptile.

How to say it

Diplodocus: say
'dih-plod-uh-kus'

Index

Notes for parents and teachers

Before reading

Ask the children to name some dinosaurs. Ask them if dinosaurs are around today. Talk about how some dinosaurs ate plants and others ate other dinosaurs. Can they think of ways these dinosaurs might have been different? Have they heard of Diplodocus? Find out what they already know about this dinosaur.

After reading

* Ask the children if they remember what a Diplodocus looked like – talk about its strong legs, long neck and long tail. Can they remember why the Diplodocus needed a long neck and tail? Give the children play dough and make models of Diplodocus.
* Choose some slow, deep music and have the children try moving like a Diplodocus. Ask the children if they think they should move slowly or quickly. How should they move their arms and legs?